SEVENTH-DAY ADVENTISTS AND THE BIBLE

Does inspiration establish authority?

An issue and a case study

EDWARD W.H. VICK

2nd Replica Edition

Energion Publications
Gonzalez, FL
2018

Copyright © 2004, Edward W. H. Vick

ISBN10: 1-63199-547-2
ISBN13: 978-1-63199-547-7
Library of Congress Control Number: 2018909383

Energion Publications
P. O. Box 841
Gonzalez, FL 32560

energion.com
pubs@energion.com

Contents

	PREFACE	iv
I	SEVENTH-DAY ADVENTISTS AND THE BIBLE	1
II	INSPIRATION AND ELLEN WHITE	13
III	IS CONCERN WITH INSPIRATION THE RIGHT CONCERN NOW?	29

Preface

This short book presents an important issue: Can inspiration establish authority? Is the question of inspiration the same as the question of authority?

The idea of inspiration has often been at the centre of attention when the Bible has been under discussion. In particular at the time of the Reformation when it was a question of defending the authority of the Bible against the claims of tradition, and in the nineteenth century discussions about science and religion. People who then defended a theory of inspiration believed very firmly that inspiration of a writing could be demonstrated. They also believed that the inspiration, so demonstrated, established the authority of the writing beyond question and that it could be established in no other way so well. No wonder they defended the doctrine of inspiration with such energy.

Our question is whether the idea of inspiration can do what its traditional proponents believed it could. Can appeal to inspiration establish the authority of the primary source, the Bible? Can it, by extension, establish the authority of a secondary source, for example the teacher, the prophet, the charismatic figure of a religious group?

Christian churches have made and continue to make such claims. So much so that we can assert that it is a widely held belief. But is it a worthy belief? Since we have now come to understand the Bible historically, can a doctrine which approaches the Bible in a non-historical way be adequate?

By taking a case study we can focus clearly issues of a general kind and hopefully by doing so, to ecclesiastical understanding. The case study is the interesting one of the Seventh-day Adventist; who as well as claiming that inspiration establishes the authority of the Bible also claims that inspiration establishes the claim of the modern prophet in that church.

The first part, about half, of the book discusses the case study. The second part considers the issue it raises as a general theological issue. What is interesting is that contemporary theological discussion, except in conservative circles, has little to say about the problem. Even to speak of inspiration is something of an anachronism. But it perhaps depends on *how* you talk about it.

I deal at greater length with issues raised here about the Bible in the book, *From Inspiration to Understanding: Reading the Bible Seriously and Faithfully*. As the title suggests, issues relating to the interpretation of the Bible are also treated.

Edward W. H. Vick
Nottingham 2004

SEVENTH-DAY ADVENTISTS AND THE BIBLE

I SEVENTH-DAY ADVENTISTS AND THE BIBLE

Seventh-day Adventists have always claimed that their 'message' is based on the Bible and that the Bible and the Bible only is the source of their doctrine and the guide of their life, as a community and as individuals. There is no doubt that it has always been the intention of the Seventh-day Adventist church to maintain and to declare that the Bible is the Christian's authority and that it is the means through which God makes known his purposes and his love to the human race, and in particular to those who respond in faith. The Holy Spirit as a present reality — and this in none other than God himself — mediates the meaning and authorizes the demands, the succour and the teachings of the Bible to the believer. In all of this Jesus Christ is centre. So in teaching what is the fundamental message of Christianity, Seventh-day Adventists identify themselves as in the Reformation tradition with its emphasis on the Bible and on faith. Authority in the church has its source in God himself who acts in the world and in the church through Word and Spirit.

Seventh-day Adventists also hold that God has revealed himself through the prophet Ellen White, and that he continues to do so. They have regard to the coming into being of a particular community in the nineteenth century, events involving a particular group of people then. They also have regard to the Seventh-day Adventist church throughout the world at the present time. In speaking of the special status of Ellen White,

Adventists point to a particular historical period, when her activities, including writing, started and became recognized, and when claims concerning her authority were popularised. They also point to a continuing event, the influence of the writings she left. In consideration of these things she has a particular authority in the church.

The reason why Ellen White has authority in the church is that Seventh-day Adventists believe that God has revealed and goes on revealing himself through her writings. Whatever God has done elsewhere and at other times, he has acted and is acting for and with this community. Seventh-day Adventists can, therefore, both explain and preserve such authority by speaking of revelation.

Such revelation and authority involve response. Both 'revelation' and 'authority' are relational terms. That means that they refer to a relation between persons. That may serve to answer the question: Why is the authority of Ellen White only acknowledged by Seventh-day Adventists among all the varied Christian churches? That is of course an important question. So it is important to find an answer. Ellen White is a corporate phenomenon. To speak of Ellen White is not to speak of an isolated individual, but of a person who has significance only within a particular group, the Seventh-day Adventist church. That means history. God has acted in the history of this church, this group. Hence the group has a continuing unity over a period of time. The group came into being and continues in being as it makes response to what it believes has been and is God's guidance. The church confesses that such guidance, such revelation has taken place and is taking place in many ways. God reveals himself through human activities and through human fallibility. The heavenly treasure is conveyed through earthly vessels.

If then Ellen White is so intimately tied to the history of this particular church that her authority is only recognised here, what is there to prevent the confession of that authority and the church itself from becoming thoroughly sectarian? Is not sectarianism precisely the claim to a special and uniquely authoritative revelation of God, one which cannot be shared with other Christians?

We have to ask, 'What *sort* of authority does Ellen White have?' The answer is that the authority here is religious, or if one prefers the term, spiritual. To have religious authority does not involve always being factually correct. Since God reveals himself through fallible human beings there is no problem whatever. One ought to have learned this long since from the discussions about the Bible that have taken place over the last hundred and fifty years. Such fallibility is not an issue and is not to be treated as if it were. In discussing Scripture the issue is authority, not the fallibility of the writings.

There is no question that Seventh-day Adventists have in the past made problematical statements about Ellen White that give the impression that this corpus of writing has priority to the Scriptures. She herself claimed that the God who then spoke in the ancient past through prophets now speaks through her. Official statements (which I have before me as I write) give all the attention to discussing the inspiration of Ellen White and none to discussing the inspiration of the Bible. Indeed, they make the experience of Ellen White the model for understanding the experience of the biblical prophet. That is to put the question quite the wrong way around. It is an *inversion* of the issue.

Seventh-day Adventists have always wished to put Jesus Christ at the centre of their life as a church. But in fact, in the working out of a doctrinal scheme, and in the attention given to Ellen White, one must raise the question. What is the relation of Ellen White to Jesus Christ? I use the term 'Ellen White' to refer sometimes to the body of writings and sometimes as well to her activities in the church and her status as she was and is acknowledged as a prophet. Sometimes I use it as a name. There will be no difficulty to understand what it means in any given instance.

God's decisive revelation is in the events the Bible records and in the life, death and resurrection of Jesus Christ. All Christian revelation has Jesus Christ as its point of reference, since God's revelation in Jesus Christ is the event from which Christians interpret all history and all experience. The problem for the Seventh-day Adventist church is to make Jesus Christ central and primary in this way in its doctrine. The problem for the theologian and for the framers of church doctrine is to interpret the Bible, life, practice, doctrine, so that the centrality and primacy of Jesus Christ comes decisively and clearly to view. What has happened in the church is that it has assumed and confessed the centrality and primacy of Jesus Christ, but has often failed to display it in its doctrine and practice. By 'practice' I mean church practice, for example its use of the written sources and the reverence given to them. Undue attention, evidenced by the sheer volume of writing, for example has been given to other issues. In particular, in the discussion of issues, writers have simply gone ahead without asking the crucial question, 'How is this discussion related to God's revelation in Jesus Christ?' That has happened, not the least, in the discussion about Ellen White. It is the task of any church calling itself Christian to discern Jesus Christ at the centre of its teaching and practice. But it must also *display* that centrality.

Seventh-day Adventists have seldom avoided the mistake of making the category of prophet dominant and all-important in the discussion of Ellen White. It is a mistake in dealing with the composition and authority of the Bible to focus exclusively upon the figure of the prophet — a serious mistake. Most of the Bible did not originate with prophets. So we have made a serious blunder if we focus on the prophet, and make the figure of the prophet the model for constructing a doctrine of Scripture. If we do so we shall, very likely, make the related mistake of giving dominance to the concept of 'inspiration.' It is not necessary, even for a theory of inspiration, to give exclusive priority to the idea of the prophet. Nor, on the other hand, do we best explain the status and authority of the biblical writings by using the concept of 'inspiration.' We can account for the great variety of writing in Scripture, confess God as source, and as active as the Scripture is now read, more adequately without such exclusive emphasis on inspiration.

This has particular relevance for discussion of Ellen White. Seventh-day Adventists have called Ellen White a prophet. There is some evidence of her reluctance to accept the title but she did not forbid it. Seventh-day Adventists have almost exclusively been content to use the idea of inspiration in the attempt to explain her status and authority in the church. The fact is that, in the construction of dogmatic theory, the idea of 'prophet' and the idea of 'inspiration' were made for each other. 'Prophet' is unduly restrictive when used of the biblical writings. 'Inspiration' is ambiguous, confusing and misleading. That is quite evident in many published discussions about the inspiration of Ellen White in Adventist literature. But it was inevitable, once Ellen White became universally acknowledged in the Adventist church as a prophet. Once the idea of inspiration had been used, it naturally led to further employment of the term.

It is not an isolated mistake however. Traditional inspiration theory of the Bible has for long made the same mistake.

To avoid sectarianism, one must avoid a preoccupation with Ellen White and a restriction of the discussion of revelation, inspiration and authority to Ellen White. One must not make reference to the Bible, when discussing these issues only because one wants to draw out a point regarding Ellen White. This can lead to extremes of argument. I give an example. The writer is attempting to establish that the inspiration of Ellen White is like that of the biblical prophet. He quotes Ellen White extensively to the effect that the prophet, in this case Moses, received a 'panoramic view' of history. She supplies in detail an account of what the prophet actually saw in his vision, in that way providing what is lacking in the Old Testament, specifically in *Deuteronomy* 34. The writer then, referring to this construction Ellen White produced, argued that Ellen White's own experience was like that of the vision she had attributed to Moses. He argues on the basis of Ellen White's construction of the visionary presentation of history to Moses that this was the way history was presented to Ellen White, giving further lengthy quotations, not from the Bible, but from Ellen White with regard to his claim.[1]

This writer explicitly stated at the outset of the article what he assumed. He starts with Ellen White and her experience, as reflected in her writing. Thereafter, we move to the Bible, the biblical figure and his experience. In doing so we confine our attention to the figure of the prophet. If we want to know about a biblical prophet, we are better off discussing Ellen White and her experience than, in the first instance, discussing the Bible.[2]

There is something quite radically wrong with this procedure. Ellen White is no exception to the rule which Seventh-day Adventists as Protestants have so firmly confessed, at least in principle, the rule *sola scriptura*. Here it is quite compromised. This procedure of special pleading, in this case arguing from Ellen White to the Bible, and supplying a supplement to the Bible to establish a crucial point about Ellen White is thoroughly sectarian. Effectively, even if that was not the author's intention, it puts the Bible in a quite subsidiary position to Ellen White.

If one is really interested in the Bible and the biblical prophet, one makes a careful comparative study of the prophets of the Bible, and then moves to discuss claims about the modern prophet.[3] But to be adequate there must be more. For, beside the fact that there are different kinds of prophet, there is also the poet, the psalmist, the wise man, the chronicler, the compiler of laws, the evangelist, the letter-writer, the apocalyptist, the historian. The prophet is one among many and the story of the 'writing' (i.e. the composition = coming into being and transmission of Scripture) has to be told in view of, and so that it can include, the many ways in which each of these thought, produced and preserved materials.

The fundamental error is to start discussion without a concern first and foremost to come to a careful and balanced understanding of the Bible. That is where other fundamentalist Christians start. We may question the adequacy of their understanding of inspiration. But there is no doubt about their obvious concern with the Bible. If the Seventh-day Adventist can get the right subject for discussion, put concern with the Bible primary, the secondary authority of Ellen White may then become clear.

So there are two concerns:

(1) The first concern is to remind the Seventh-day Adventist of the Protestant heritage and to urge that consideration of authority begin with the Bible, and that such study be done with historical understanding.

(2) The second concern is to question whether to use the idea and to develop a doctrine of inspiration is the best procedure. Ask, in all seriousness, Are you sure that the idea of inspiration can establish the authority of the Bible? Obviously if it can't establish the authority of the Bible, it cannot establish the authority of secondary writings.

In examining the evidence from Scripture we must first of all recognize that there are many, many kinds of writing there. These varied writings come from a variety of circumstances, were written for very different purposes, had very varied audiences in the first instance. We take into account the many kinds of functionary represented in the Bible. There are many kinds of person behind the Scriptures, not only the prophet.

The Seventh-day Adventist must come to terms with such questions as these: How did God reveal himself through the limitations of human beings at specific points in human history? What sort of book is the Bible? What kind of authority does the Bible have for God to reveal himself through it, through its limitations and errors?

This will mean putting questions in order of importance, so that the real issues are thoroughly discussed. To give an example: It is not an issue whether the Bible resulted from a long historical process in which there was borrowing, copying, editing, revising, collection, rejection and acceptance of writings.

Similarly, it is not an issue whether Ellen White is sometimes in error, that Ellen White resulted from a process in which there was borrowing, copying, editing, revising, collection of writings, rejection and acceptance. We cannot establish the authority of Ellen White by asserting a theory of her inspiration, any more than we can do for the Bible.

What *is* at issue is the question of the authority of the Bible. In what does that authority consist? How can we most adequately discuss this? Not, we shall hold, on the basis of a theory of inspiration, since even a more adequate theory of inspiration cannot establish the authority of the writings claimed to be inspired. That authority is the authority of the living and acting God who now makes himself known in Jesus Christ through the Holy Spirit.

The Seventh-day Adventist speaks a great deal about truth. The understanding of what authority and what truth is, is therefore crucial. It is essential to get the right perspective here. The problem of authority will emerge as an important question in this book. We must so define truth that the definition takes account of the fact that the living God is dealing with us in our history. We must not so define truth that we can, as it were, capture God in our propositions.

Notes

[1] A.L.White, *Toward a Factual Concept of Inspiration.* Mimeographed Article. Washington D.C. February 10 1967. pp. 10-11.

[2] *Ibid.,* pp. 2-3.

[3] Niels-Erik Andreasen, 'From Vision to Prophecy.' *Adventist Review,* January 28, 1982, pp. 4(76) - 7(79) examines carefully, and with historical sensitivity, the Old Testament book of Amos. He asks the question, 'Is there a relationship, and if so what is it, between the prophet's vision and the prophet's message?' That article at least represents a beginning. We at least start with the biblical data. Adventist scholars of the Bible might well draw on the wealth of materials available from biblical scholars, and let the great variety of literature in the Bible receive attention as the question of biblical authority is raised within the Adventist church. It is not so much the scale of the study but the perspective and the perspicacity that matters. In drawing upon the

common resources of Christian scholarship, Seventh-day Adventists might better understand and reshape their own context, and the form, of the questions which emerge from it.

II INSPIRATION AND ELLEN WHITE

This chapter will make some observations about articles which Seventh-day Adventist writers have produced. It will conclude with remarks of a general sort and a statement of issues needing clarification.

We begin with a short article proposing inspiration and, in particular, revelation as important issues. The gist of the argument is that there are two alternative views of revelation, one of which is the right one. 'Revelation is the communication of God addressed to the human mind in conceptual messages and in actions that require conceptual understanding.'[2] The second, which the author attacks, he defines simply as 'a personal encounter with God.'[2] He proposes that revelation is 'inscripturated' in the Bible. It is there whether anybody finds it or not. 'The Bible is the depository of revealed truth, given once and for all.' So there, in the Bible, you have a statement of normative truth. It is 'objective' in the sense that it is there, whether anyone accepts it or not, whether anyone has an encounter with God or not. This leads to the astonishing claim, 'biblical revelation is not affected by any personal encounter with God.'[3] Revelation is in propositional terms.' This ensures that it is rational and precise. So 'the understanding of revelation is arrived at through ideas.'[4]

The article is brief and the author does not tell us about the process whereby the reader or interpreter comes to understand the ideas of the Bible in such a way that no misunderstanding or subjectivity enters into the 'reception of the revelation.' But that *is* a primary question. 'How should the Bible be interpreted?' The question demands an appropriate answer. Otherwise the claim about the objectivity of the revelation becomes abstract and empty.

The article represents an oversimplification of the issues. There are not just two ways of defining revelation. We are here given an 'either-or;' and we must choose. Either 'propositional revelation' or what the article calls, rather misleadingly, 'existential encounter.' The exposition claims that these are polar opposites and suggests no alternative. It then calls the 'propositional revelation' objective, and the so-called existential view subjective. The objective is good. The subjective is bad. But I have never been quite sure what the target of the writer's criticism of subjective, existential revelation is. It appears to be a generalisation based on an interpretation of theologians such as Brunner, Bultmann and Barth. But that is puzzling. Brunner was very firm against subjectivism. He also was very firm against an opposition between objective and subjective. He calls such dualism 'this fatal antithesis' and argues at length against it.[5] Barth, above all, wished to preserve the 'objectivity' of God's revelation. Bultmann agreed with Barth about God's otherness, but insisted that revelation is abstract unless it is related to human experience, unless we speak about the human experience of God and the change in our understanding which it brings about.

The following questions arise in relation to this theory:

(1) Is 'objectivity' a clear enough idea to be serviceable? May what is to be 'objective' in fact be highly 'subjective'?

(2) What does 'propositional' mean? What is a proposition? What is propositional revelation? Should the church treat the Bible as a collection of rational propositions? What would happen if it did?

(3) What possibilities are there for other definitions of revelation? What definitions have Christian writers given to the term 'revelation'?

The opposition suggested is over simple and misleading. The terms 'objective' and 'subjective' cannot help us in careful definition of these issues. The concept of revelation, when duly defined and carefully explained, is a very suggestive and helpful concept. In due course we shall examine it at some length.

The article remains content to make a distinction between two views of revelation. What is now needed is a systematic statement, providing an adequate understanding of revelation and connecting a definition of revelation with other issues such as inspiration, authority, canonicity and history. In short, the concept of revelation needs to be related to a theology of Bible and of church. Please note that in a short, popular treatise such as I intend this book to be, I can only make a beginning.

A concept of revelation will not stand by itself, isolated. It is easy to make assertions. It is the more difficult task of theology to produce a systematic account relating such definitions and assertions to the whole range of Christian ideas. I shall, in what follows, make an introductory attempt to relate the idea of revelation to the problems which I have summarized in these introductory chapters. I believe that in doing so a whole range of questions which Seventh-day Adventists have been asking can be addressed. Two results will follow: First, some of those problems and questions hitherto given prominence will drop away as misleading or irrelevant. Second, we shall see that some purported answers are simply assertions without evidence, and others are over-simplifications of the problems. It is one thing to criticise, to produce a sheaf of quotations, to provide a few emphatic sentences of assertion. It is quite another thing to construct.

At times there has been a movement in some Seventh-day Adventist circles towards a kind of theological questioning. But little theological construction has emerged from the questioning. I refer for example to a *Spectrum* article[6] in which the author, rightly to my mind, holds the following positions: (1) Ellen White's use of sources, the failure of her assistants sometimes to disclose sources and leaders' questionable use of Ellen White's authority to maintain control of the church are irrelevant for determining the 'prophetic status' of Ellen White. Critical questioning should not disturb us. We do not have to be worried about such critical questioning, if we understand aright. (2) We must deal 'reverently yet honestly with . . . the Bible.'

The subject of discussion about authority should be the Bible. Having come to an adequate understanding here, the problem of the authority of secondary writings will largely disappear. Many years ago, I wrote to a colleague and said that I hoped the discussion about Ellen White which was beginning to take place would make it possible for the Seventh-day Adventist church to come to terms with serious and critical discussion, followed by constructive theology with respect to the Bible. Perhaps that may now be beginning to happen in the Adventist church.

The *Spectrum* article assumed that the way to continue discussion is by deploying the idea of inspiration. If only we go on talking about 'inspiration' but in the right way, we will come to an adequate understanding. So the author talks about the Bible as 'the one document that we all agree is the foundation for any theory of inspiration' (51), and commends the viewpoint: 'retain the human element in *inspiration*' and 'not allow humanity (i.e. the fact that the writer was human) rob an *inspired* word of its divine power'(52).

The article simply accepts that the discussion must be about inspiration. There is no doubt here that inspiration will be the central and key concept. Perhaps that is the root of the problem. My suggestion is that, while there are worse and better ways of speaking about inspiration and while Seventh-day Adventists search for better ways, there are very serious limitations to the concept itself. These render it inadequate to account for the authority of the Bible, in view of historical, literary and scientific analysis. If the concept of inspiration cannot account for the authority of the Bible, it is *a fortiori* inadequate to account for the authority of secondary sources.

In the task of reconstruction we must be prepared to deploy an extended vocabulary, as well as give attention to different perspectives. What sometimes happens in church discussions is that ideas once given prominence come to be seen as relatively unimportant. Conversely, it also happens that developments take place when ideas which have not been given prominence are seen to be more important than previously was thought.

A further article[7], accompanying the one from which we have just quoted makes two observations which we might well explore. First, that 'an artificial and misplaced sense of uniqueness can accrue to religious (and other) writings over a period of time' especially if few questions about them get asked. The second point is also important. Religious writings are still known to us because the church considers them 'from the outset special and worth preserving.' 'The point is that inspired texts are with us . . . by means of canonization.'[8]

This raises a serious question. It is obvious once it is pointed out. Why did the church consider those writings it preserved worth preserving? Now you cannot have it both ways. I think it is confusing to say, 'Inspired texts are with us because the church thought they were worth preserving.' Why not leave out the idea of inspiration and simply say, 'The church thought these writings worth preserving?' Then one can go on and say why the church thought them worth preserving. Some answers to that question are better than others, and the official answers are sometimes not the right ones.

What is certain and should be a central consideration is that those writings were used in the church and had influence in the church, with little concern, at first, about how they came to be written or put together. The church gave them a special status by its use of them. The church recognized that they had a special status. When it wanted to defend that status, against attack and against alternative views, it then *and only then* developed and deployed a theory of inspiration. Such a theory developed only centuries later as Reformers came to terms with the alternative Catholic theory of tradition.

Construction of a theory of inspiration is an attempt to defend the status the writings already have. It is a way of defending the act of having accepted the writings as having authority. They do not have the status because they are inspired. They have that status because they have been accepted and are being used by the church. Talk about inspiration *follows* such acceptance, remembering and continuing acknowledgement. That is why it is confusing to say, 'inspired texts are with us by means of canonisation.' Any text would be. If the clause quoted means that certain texts have authority which others do not have because the church has accepted them and uses them and experiences the revelation of God through them, that is alright. But we confuse the issue by introducing the ambiguous term 'inspiration' here.

Perhaps it would conduce to clarity if we were to address such questions as these. Is a writing accepted because it has the feature of 'being inspired'? Or, is it 'inspired' because it is accepted? Are there writings which are 'inspired' but not accepted? Are all writings accepted 'inspired'? 'Accepted' means being used and having authority.

From time to time articles in Seventh-day Adventist journals discuss the question of history, historical sources, the writer's integrity, with particular reference to Ellen White.

Historical statements are statements about the past for which there is evidence. The difference between history and fiction is that there is evidence for the historical account. Whether, having produced the evidence, the account will be adequate is a further question. One of the features of good history writing besides style is that it draws from primary sources. Mediocre history writing is content with secondary sources. It was a great achievement of the nineteenth century to develop a historical method and a historical consciousness. It was a great achievement of Christians that they participated in these concerns. That participation required clear thinking and adjustment of previously held positions.

Ellen White's book, *The Great Controversy* makes sweeping surveys of centuries of events. We now hear that it does not matter that aspects of the account are not historically trustworthy, that it contains factual errors. The account was constructed by wholesale quotation and went through several editings in which other people than the named author made their contributions. Seventh-day Adventists now realize that these things must be taken into account when they speak of 'inspiration.' Biblical scholars have known this for over a century and have discussed the adequacy of the idea of inspiration in view of such facts, in relation to the Bible.

Ellen White claimed to have had visions of the events she wrote about. For an historical assessment of the writing, however, there are agreed upon rules, and in writing out historical events she was in the province of the historian. Such writing is historically worthy provided there is evidence for the accounts given, the events described, and provided that the writing represents the facts correctly. But, we might ask, What relevance does an historical assessment have in relation to the claim that a document has religious or spiritual authority?

It is quite consistent to say that while there is error in the accounts, and while there was wholesale borrowing, the writing has authority. This is so whether one talks of inspiration or not. The question is, Does God reveal himself in the writings and, if so, to whom? Ask that question of the Bible and the answer is that God reveals himself to the Christian through the Bible. The Christian responds. Ask the question of Ellen White and the Seventh-day Adventist should reply, God reveals himself to the Adventist through Ellen White. The Lutheran could say that of Martin Luther, and other churches of the writings of other people, all the while recognizing the Bible as primary.

Much Seventh-day Adventist writing and deployment of ideas on the problem of inspiration and authority strikes one as being *ad hoc*. It seems to be assumed that one ought to use the idea of inspiration, and that one must use the model of the prophet to explain why it is that Ellen White had and has authority. But why does one make these two assumptions? It would seem to be time to examine what one means by 'authority' and 'having authority', and having done that, then ask whether the idea of inspiration, and the use of the prophet as the norm of inspiration, is fitting. Most Seventh-day Adventists want to address these questions in the first instance to the problem of Ellen White. But one should here be rather patient and *first* think of the Bible. One should discuss the adequacy of the concepts of inspiration, prophet, revelation, and authority to explain the place the Bible has in the church. Then,

Seventh-day Adventists can proceed to discuss Ellen White in view of the conclusions arrived at in relation to the Bible.

We might proceed by examining, even if briefly, the way in which our topic has been treated by significant writers before and contemporary with us. In the case of 'inspiration' we can examine the main lines of definition from the Reformation to the present without too great difficulty. The materials are readily available. Again, it is a matter of being patient. We must sharpen our tools before we can use them well. To change the metaphor, we can draw upon the plan of the major definitions and discussions before we tackle the topic of inspiration and Ellen White.

In what follows in this writing I shall examine the major definitions of inspiration in Christian theology. I shall then explain why such definitions and such accounts are inadequate. I shall then suggest an alternative. One of the conclusions I shall draw as the result of this study is this: *'inspiration' is an inadequate concept to expound the claim that Scripture has authority.* That means that it is inadequate and misleading to argue: The Bible is inspired. Therefore, the Bible had authority. Therefore the Bible should be followed in responsive obedience.

The authority religious writings have has to do with the continuing acceptance of them and the continuing use of them. If the biblical writings were not held in esteem they would have no authority, even if they had been inspired. Religious books have their unique authority only as God reveals himself through them. So the Bible has authority, not in and of itself, but only as its constituent writings are the instruments of God's revelation.

An essential part of our discussion will be to define the meaning and, if possible, clear away ambiguity in the terms at the heart of the matter, namely, 'inspiration,' 'authority,' and 'revelation.'

Seventh-day Adventists discussed these problems in very simple terms. For, in the formative years of the church the leaders were not theologically sophisticated. Indeed, there persists still to the present an anxiety and a fear of theology and of philosophy. Those leaders, convinced that the Holy Spirit was leading them, impressed by the activities of Ellen White and the claims she and others were making, tried, within the compass of a narrow range of ideas, to explain what it all meant. They tried to keep what appeared to be disturbing questions within limits, but also at the same time to come to a fuller understanding. For example the 1919 debate moved within a rather narrow set of ideas, but questions were then asked and perspectives were expressed which, if they had been followed up, would have saved much of the late problematic. For example, G.B.Thompson with insight proposed: 'the evidence of the inspiration of the Testimonies is not in their verbal inspiration, but in their influence and power in the denomination.'[9] That is not well expressed, since the term 'inspiration' is used twice and is doing double service, but it is reasonably clear what he meant. He further said, 'It was not whether it was verbally inspired or not, but it carried the power of the Spirit of God with it.'[10] The writings had authority not because of their 'inspiration' but because God revealed himself through them. Then too, if the discerning questions of B.L.House had really been pursued, while there may have been immediate heart searching and confusion, much needless authoritarianism would no doubt have been avoided.

We must say something similar about attempts at explanation which had their source in the Ellen G. White Estate. One article very earnestly attempts to explain the authority of Ellen White in terms of her inspiration, but because of limited concepts and restricted theological knowledge is not able to clarify the issues where light most needs to be shed. The articles have such a dominating interest in Ellen White that they make the primary question that of the inspiration of Ellen White, and to make subsidiary what should be the primary question, of the inspiration and authority of the Bible. But if that is what happens, then the claim to authority for Ellen White and the explanation and defence of that authority becomes unprotestant and sectarian. A writing on the defensive and with a limited range of ideas as well as an ecclesiastically introversive attitude tends to resort to dubious arguments. There is a constant quoting of Ellen White even about Ellen White's inspiration and authority when these are the very problems in question, rather than a coming to terms with the issue for the church and for theology: On what basis do Seventh-day Adventists acknowledge Ellen White's authority? Is it adequate to use the idea of inspiration to defend that acknowledgment? No amount of exposition of what Ellen White says about inspiration can clarify the issue when the issue is to explain the very grounds for saying Ellen White is inspired. You cannot quote claims and arguments from the writings in question as a basis for claiming either inspiration or authority when the very things are in question. One has to start at a more fundamental level.

Please note that we are not, on principle, doubting assumptions when we ask what they mean and whether there are reasonable grounds for holding them. Certainly we have no desire to question the sincerity and fervour with which people hold such convictions. But if we are going to be clear we must probe in the way we are suggesting.

We ask for the same acknowledgement of our sincerity also, and at the same time a fair discussion of the issues with which we are dealing. The more adequate the range of ideas, and the more clearly and unambiguously and relevantly we define our ideas the more satisfactory will be the resulting treatment. So we shall aim for clear definition and for clear relationships between relevant ideas.

We conclude the chapter with a few questions and a few answers.

What is added to the *content* of Ellen White if one holds that the writings are inspired? What would be lost from the content of Ellen White if one did not hold the writings to be inspired? What would be lost from the authority of Ellen White if one did not hold Ellen White to have been inspired? This question does *not* mean, 'What, at least for many Seventh-day Adventists, would be a condition for accepting the writings as authoritative?

Ellen White would have the same authority as now if the visions and messages were not divinely given, (1) provided they were believed to have been divinely given and (2) provided that the writings were read, accepted and had influence.

Of late some Seventh-day Adventists are making a distinction where previously no such distinction was made. It is the distinction between the historical writings and the Testimonies, although it is interesting to notice that people were aware of this as far back as 1919. Perhaps this will lead to a complication, namely that of distinguishing a primary and secondary Ellen White! But the long failure to make such a distinction illustrates the point I am now making. That point is that as long as all the writings were believed to have been divinely inspired and divinely imparted, no distinction was drawn between them, they were all considered equally authoritative, even if they were very different writings.

So we must ask the question. Why are these writings said to be divinely given? Seventh-day Adventists resist the answer in terms of psychological phenomena sociologically appropriate at the point in history when Ellen White lived. It is of course a fact that Adventists have appealed to the abnormal psychological states of Ellen White as evidence for her messages being divinely given. Even were a psychological and sociological explanation given — and in due course they will be — Seventh-day Adventists would go on insisting on a religious and theological explanation. It is a fact that the psychological and physical phenomena associated with the condition of Ellen White were, for some of her observers, directly and positively related to the claim of divine origin. Most Adventists have heard the arguments from the unusual phenomena (for example, 'She does not breathe' and the holding up of a heavy Bible and the pointing out of texts in it, the seeing of visions of places she later identified,) to the 'inspiration' of Ellen White, and to the divine origin of (all) the messages written and orally delivered, and thence to their authority.

We can spell out the argument. It runs:

Unusual phenomena accompany Ellen White.
Such unusual phenomena have a divine source.
So, Ellen White has a divine source.

That, however, is an invalid argument. So, because it is unsound, further deductions (to inspiration and authority of Ellen White) cannot be properly drawn from it. The argument is invalid, to whomever it is applied. This should be clear when it is put in its general form, namely:

Unusual phenomena have a divine source.
Such unusual phenomena sometimes accompany a person who makes religious claims.
Therefore, those claims are thereby shown to be valid.

Since that is patently an unsound argument, it will have to be explained why, if it is made in a particular case, anyone should then accept it as a persuasive piece of reasoning.

Notes

[1] Edward Heppenstall, 'Doctrine of Revelation and Inspiration,' *The Ministry*. July 1970. pp. 16-19 The author was a teacher at the Seventh-day Adventist Theological Seminary for many years. This article is thus a summary of this aspect of seminary theology, and

of what Seventh-day Adventist ministers heard for a generation about the Bible.

[2] *Ibid.*, p. 16.
[3] *Ibid.*, p. 17.
[4] *Ibid.* p. 16.
[5] Emil Brunner, *The Divine Human Encounter.* Translated by Amandus VT. Loos. Philadelphia: The Westminster Press, 1943. p. 29. Brunner speaks very emphatically against the opposition of these two types of revelation. He wrote,

'The fact remains that in faith we are dealing, not with truths, not even with divinely revealed truths, but with God, with Jesus Christ, with the Holy Spirit. . . .but this personal happening is indissolubly linked with conceptual content, with truth in the general sense of the word, truth as doctrine, knowledge as perception of facts. God gives himself to us in no other way than that he says something to us, namely the truth about himself.' *Ibid.*, pp. 111-112.

[6] Alden Thompson, 'The Imperfect Speech of Inspiration,' *Spectrum*. Vol. 12. Number 4. pp. 48-55.

[7] Jonathan Butler, 'Prophet or Plagiarist: A False Dichotomy,' *Ibid.*, pp. 45-48.

[8] *Ibid.*, p. 47.

[9] Reported in *Spectrum*, Volume 10. Number 1, p. 49.

[10] *Ibid.*, p. 50.

[11] These observations relate in particular to the following articles: Arthur L. White, *The Vital Importance of an Understanding of Inspiration.* 1958, and *Toward a Factual Concept of Inspiration* 1967. Washington D.C.: Ellen G. White Estate.

III IS CONCERN WITH INSPIRATION THE RIGHT CONCERN NOW?

There are different *kinds of concern*. Note three. First, there is the antiquarian, or the historical concern. This is about what happened, the events, ideas and teachings of yesterday. Its interest is not in whether or not they may have relevance or currency in the present. Such historical concern may take into account the influence past teachings have had as thinking has developed. The second kind of concern is to repeat, to rework, to rehabilitate the idea or teaching. The third kind of concern is constructive: to *move* forward, having been instructed by the lessons we may have learnt from past teachings, debates and conclusions.

We may also distinguish two *levels of concern*: involved concern and analytical, critical concern. These are not incompatible. Sometimes people engage in analytical work because they have little or no personal involvement with the questions with which they deal, but then sometimes because they are passionately concerned.

Our concern here is to stand back and examine what people were concerned to achieve with the problem of inspiration and authority and to ask the question, 'Was such involved concern that people had about inspiration appropriate and fruitful?' So we shall ask critical questions.

Historical and questioning concern may serve the constructive task of theology. We will not take for granted that the problem should be discussed in the traditional style. We shall see and note the limits of previous discussions. This will enable us to instruct those who have not yet, even after a hundred and fifty years, become aware of the course of the discussion. One might express the sanguine hope that once such issues become clear, we can then move forward to a more adequate theology. It is certainly time to move beyond the nineteenth century!

A further way of distinguishing concerns is to point out that they have particular contexts, grow out of particular historical conditions, and are for particular purposes. An ecclesiastical concern is not always identical with an academic concern. We may wish to separate and isolate church theology from academic theology. But that is not always possible. Academic questions have a way of showing up in the church context, perhaps decades later. An issue which has previously been thoroughly discussed academically may finally become the subject of church interest and concern. The church is sometimes forced into noticing it because questions will persist. Now, in such a case the church, if it will, may inherit the earlier discussions and benefit from past debates, pick up the conclusions and arguments and move forward. The church does not have to start from scratch, as if nothing had ever been discussed except what had been said in the narrower church context.

Meanwhile theological discussion moves on, and the old concerns have given place to new ones. So concern with the old question, in this case with inspiration, *might* become anachronistic and not illuminating for the present in any positive way.

Tension, if not conflict, then takes place between the academic and the churchman.

This shows itself in the opposition of church doctrine to theological innovation, even when such innovation is constructive. The theologian is sometimes caught between two poles and must sometimes balance interests without becoming schizophrenic. An important issue is at stake. Should one be concerned with the preservation of a structure of authority if to do so requires the revival of positions and the repetition of discussions long since debated and shown to be unsatisfactory? Part of the problem is that theological construction, which may require critical assessments, may not be seen to be helpful.

Part of the equipment of an intelligent Christian is the knowledge of the important debates of Christian history. History sometimes repeats itself when people try to reproduce those anachronistic positions, as if they had not been vigorously debated in the past, as if, for example, one might simply repeat traditional inspiration theory after the nineteenth century discussions. Such concern is irrelevant and wasteful. Reference to such past discussion is profitable only if it leads to construction.

Since it is appropriate to correct error, to moderate exaggeration, to call attention to what is anachronistic, to point out aberration, the concern we are showing here may prove to be relevant. If, for example, the construction of a theory of inspiration is an error of judgment as well as unsatisfactory theology, it is worthwhile to point that out.

Objection is raised that such approaches are 'negative and critical.' But that can hardly be taken seriously as an objection. If we negate misleading or erroneous teaching and thinking that can only be to the good. If we then try to construct, that should be welcomed or at least be worthy of serious consideration and discussion. Often those who criticize constructive theology are themselves paradigm examples of the negative and critical attitude. Nothing is more negative than to dismiss out of hand, as it were on principle.

The very basic positions to be explained in what follows are: (1) that a theology of inspiration has nothing of substance to contribute to a system of doctrine; (2) that a theology of inspiration does not establish the authority of the writing for which inspiration is claimed; and (3) that it is a serious mistake to emphasise the inspiration of the Bible by setting the Bible in opposition to tradition. 'The Bible and the Bible only' (*sola scriptura*) and 'Scripture and tradition' are not contradictory but complementary ideas.

What seems irrelevant for one concern may seem highly relevant for another. The theologian is sometimes torn between the academic and the church problem. One wishes to be honest and scholarly and one wishes to have approval. One knows that it is anachronistic to engage in such debate. One also knows that the church is widely and often emotionally concerned in debating the issue.

Concern with the problem of inspiration in the Seventh-day Adventist context has a peculiar significance. Ellen White is identified as a prophet, and various reasons are given for this identification. To be a prophet, God must inspire. When God inspires, the person and the product, the prophet's speech and writing, has authority. Then the Adventist moves from the modern prophet's inspiration and authority to those of the Bible and employs the norms developed in relation to the modern prophet to the Bible, having already drawn selectively from the Bible to 'establish' the status of the prophet. It is to be noted and questioned and not simply assumed that in discussing the question of inspiration the prophet is to be taken as the model of the process and product of inspiration.

This example illustrates our point about different types of concern. One type, concerned with the tradition, insists that the traditional teachings be repeated, defended and refurbished. The other type is ready to entertain such questions as the following. (1) Why single out the figure of the prophet as the model for inspiration? Why not the historian, the apostle, or the redactor, or all of them? No one of these has more importance than the other. (2) Why assume that a person who is inspired has authority? Why assume that an inspired person's writings have authority? (3) The movement from modern prophet to Bible is surely wrong? The movement should be from Bible to modern prophet! But that opens up the problem on a more fundamental level. Why the fascination with the category of prophet? (4) What is there to learn from the discussions of the last two hundred years concerning the Bible? Protestant theology has long since moved on to other problems than inspiration.

Here are two categorical assertions.

First, if the only interest in discussing inspiration is to demonstrate the authority of the Bible then it is not a proper concern.

Second, It is misguided to maintain the inerrancy of Scripture. To establish *per impossible* that the Bible did not err on matters of fact would not establish its authority as a religious or, spiritual document. Nor, conversely to display that it was fallible would overthrow such religious authority. Here the very idea of inerrancy is a mistake and an irrelevance, and has misled generations of Christians.

The Reformers used the language of dictation, but the Bible was not for them a body of propositions which had come into being as a result of a process of verbal inspiration, as the earlier metaphors of God using men as his pen or his lyre suggested. Such figures of speech appeared in the early days of the church. But no doctrine of inspiration was developed then. That only came into being after the Reformation.

What was important for both Luther and Calvin was the way in which the Bible actually functioned in the living process of witnessing to faith and of creating faith in the church. There was serious retrogression when the Protestant Scholastics made the Bible a book that was inspired down to the letter and therefore was inerrant in the sense that whatever it claims about whatever subject could not in fact be faulted. The stress upon the infallible church was met by the assertion of an infallible book. This new doctrine of inspiration was designed to meet the situation in which objective certainty was required by a church which had no infallible teaching office.

However it is misleading to set the Protestant doctrine of inspiration, and its accompanying *Sola*

Seventh-Day Adventists and the Bible 35

Scriptura in opposition to the Catholic teaching concerning inspiration and the accompanying doctrine of tradition. There is agreement between Catholic and Protestant. Trent (1546) declared that the written books of Scripture contain saving truth. The Westminster Confession (1645) spoke of God as the author of Scripture and declared that everything needful for faith and life could be found in Scripture or deduced from it. When the Enlightenment proposed a reassessment of God's relation to the world, both of these classical models were shaken to their very foundations .[1]

Conservative evangelical teaching concerning inspiration consists of the following propositions. The Bible contains no error, is infallible. Inspiration extends to the words of Scripture and is (in some sense) verbal. The Bible claims to be inerrant and authoritative. The Bible is inerrant because it is inspired and because it claims to be inspired. God imparted the Scripture to the writer — whether by 'dictation'; or not.[2] The result is true doctrine. God communicates true doctrine to human beings. The Bible is inspired means the Bible has divine authority.

Inspiration theory singles out for particular emphasis the process of the writing down of the text. It is the 'writer' who is inspired. But that is simplistic. The production of Scripture from the earliest emergence of tradition to the acceptance of books on a list (= canon) is however an extremely complex process. The writing down of the book is one stage in the process. For example with regard to the Gospels we can discern four stages — and be it noted, the model of the prophet does not apply here — (1) the formation of tradition(s), for example the circulation of stories about Jesus and their connection with problems of the church several decades before writing is produced; (2) the preservation of such traditions, for example the passing on of the stories by word of mouth; (3) the 'writing,' i.e. the committing of the traditions to a written form; (4) the acceptance of such tradition, now written, as Scripture.

It is important to notice that inspiration theory focuses on one part of the total process namely the writing but that is the part of the total process we cannot always identify. To account adequately for the Bible we must look at the whole process. An assessment of inspiration theory must take into account its partiality. Its interest is truncated, limited.

In what follows we are speaking of inspiration as a theory, as a systematic account purporting to establish the reliability, trustworthiness and authority of the Bible.

The theory of inspiration is not a fundamental nor a substantive doctrine. There would be no change whatever in a set of teachings based on the Bible if a theory of inspiration were lacking. Not a single doctrine depends upon the theory of inspiration. The question of inspiration is as though of no importance for the interpreter of Scripture. If Christian teaching is true, its truth does not depend upon a theory of inspiration. Such a theory is dispensable. If we were to drop out inspiration, no other doctrine would go, since no other doctrine hangs on it. Even B.B. Warfield recognised that.[3] The interpreter can for all intents and purposes ignore theories of inspiration. The reason is very simple. The task of the interpreter is to get at and to display the meaning of what was written. That does not require the interpreter to endorse a particular theory how what was written came to be written. The function of a theory of inspiration lies somewhere else.

A theory of inspiration does not establish the authority of Scripture nor of doctrines based upon it. Specifically the statement, 'The Bible is inspired' and the statement 'The Bible has authority' are not equivalent. This is not hard to show. 'The Bible is inspired' means that it was brought into being as the result of a particular process and that it has a quality that results from the process which brought it into being. But authority is *not* a quality anything can have in and of itself. Authority is relational. That means that something or someone has authority *for* someone. Authority is not an intrinsic property of books, say their infallibility or inerrancy. Writings have authority for someone within a particular, i.e. social and historical, context. A book, a person, or an institution without influence is without authority. Recognition of authority is a social fact.

So, since the two statements are not equivalent, there must be some logical connection between them if they are to be used together. In other words, the two statements that follow constitute an argument, i.e. a process of thought where one statement or a set of statements form the grounds for concluding, i.e. inferring, the truth of another. In a deductive argument the premises provide the grounds for the conclusion.

The Bible is inspired.

Therefore, the Bible has authority.

Now an argument is either valid or invalid. This argument is invalid. This means that the statement 'The Bible has authority' does not follow from the claim that the Bible is inspired, even if the claim that the Bible is inspired is true, and the conclusion is also true. Of course this does not mean that the statement, 'The Bible has authority' is false. It simply means that it does not follow from the statement, 'The Bible is inspired.' You cannot deduce authority from inspiration.

What seems to have taken place is this. First, one establishes that a writing *was* inspired. This means finding and exhibiting evidence that in the process of composition, the divine influenced the human in a remarkable way. Then one makes the next move. The writing was inspired, so the writing *is* inspired. What that means is something very different however. To say, 'The writing *is* inspired' means that it should be taken as primary influence in the worship, the doctrine and the act of the community. It should be allowed to exercise influence. It should be granted priority over all other sources.

Notice the basic ambiguity or equivocation of the term 'inspired.' Put simply, one is making an inference from 'the writer was inspired' (=was divinely influenced) to 'the writing is inspired' (= should be given special attention, has authority). That inference is unwarranted. It assumes that the two meanings of 'inspired' can be conflated. They cannot.

Usually the argument is extended. The following explication (of what is very often implicated in Christian claims about Christian teaching) shows how:

(1) The writers of the Bible were inspired (past tense).

(2) The Bible is inspired (present tense).

(3) Therefore the Bible has authority

(4) Therefore its teachings are true.

(5) Therefore *this* system of teachings is true and has authority, because based on the Bible.

(6) Therefore this system of teachings ought to be believed and acted upon as God's truth.

The argument is both complex and unsound. The key terms are equivocal. Each of these terms needs extended discussion, e.g. inspired, Bible, authority, interpretation, 'based on.' Here, for example, are questions we must clarify.

Why, in speaking of the Bible should we refer to sixty-six books, rather than sixty-four, or seventy? Who made that decision, and why should we follow it? Why should I simply accept it? If I accept it, I follow tradition. This is the question of the canon.

What precisely does 'having authority' mean?

In what senses historically, geographically, philosophically, scientifically, are what these writings teach true? Are the many doctrines of God taught in different parts of the Bible true? Or, is the truth that, at some time or other, people believed them to be true, e.g. Jephtha, Gideon, Jeremiah, Job's friends, Jesus, Paul?

How, in view of such diversity of teaching based on the Bible can we be sure that we are interpreting adequately? In short, what does it mean to say that a teaching is 'based on' the Bible. To the question, 'How does one relate the text of Scripture to the modern reader?' one answer often given is that one *translates* the text. But is the idea of interpretation as 'translating the text' correct? There are many difficulties in thinking of this as the task of biblical, let alone, of systematic theology. It is not simply a matter of providing a correct translation of sentences in an ancient language into a modern one. It is not always a simple matter to provide the meaning of the text for the modern reader. This is evident when divergent renderings of meaning take place from a given text. What is the point of claiming the Bible is without error if different and contradictory teachings follow from it when we interpret it?

How does one make the move from the extrinsic authority of the Bible, to the ethical obligation of belief and action? Surely not by a process of logical deduction, for the argument is a deductive one. We should act on principles deduced from the Bible's having been inspired?

The fact is that in the life of the church we consider some writings to be more important than others. Some we quite overlook, and think no more about the fact that this is what we are doing. It is the same with the forming of a church's doctrine. Construction of ecclesiastical doctrines on the basis of Scripture is *always* selective.

We can show that the initial argument is invalid very simply.

(1) Suppose that the collection of writings which was initially produced as the inspiration theory suggests, (by writers having words or thoughts divinely supplied to their minds and preserved in the writings) was never read. An unread writing has no authority. To have authority it must have influence. The collection may never be read. A writing in a collection may never be read. So an inspired writing can be without authority, by not being read, by not having influence.

The corollary to this is that a writing which is not 'inspired' (in the sense we have been examining) may have authority. It has authority as it is used in a particular way, whether it was (is) inspired or not. It has authority if it provides grounds for doctrines people actually believe. It has authority if and as it provides grounds and incentives for acts people actually do. It has authority in that it functions to maintain community and to change people's attitudes and lives. It has authority if it is *functional.* An uninspired writing may have more influence than an inspired writing. Whether any writing or pronouncement has authority depends upon the extent of its use and influence, upon the fact that responses are made to what it says. Such responses may vary. In some cases there will be discussion that leads to disagreement.

(2) What then is the point of the traditional theory of inspiration? Can we specify the function of that theory? The answer is that it functions in fact as a rationalisation. The function of the theory is something other than *to provide grounds for its conclusion*, i.e. that the Bible has authority. Inspiration theory developed to support positions already held, to fortify attitudes already present, to authorise a system. In particular the elaborate inspiration theory developed, mistakenly, to fortify the principle of *sola scriptura.* This was in opposition to the principle of 'Scripture and Tradition.' The rationale is clear. The inspiration of the Bible guarantees its sole unique authority in opposition to the contrary claim that tradition, council or Pope are fundamental authorities. Traditional inspiration theory provided a rationalisation for the proposition that what the Bible taught (i.e. Reformation theology) was to be preferred to what non-biblical sources taught (Catholic teaching). It may be a defensible position that teachings based on the Bible are to be preferred to truths not based

on the Bible. But to try to show this by developing a theory of inspiration turned out to be dubious, suspect, irrational. Inspiration theory becomes the big red herring of Christian theology.

(3) Now to our third thesis. The traditional doctrine of inspiration is ambiguous, confused, and unable to explain important facts about Scripture. To mention specific points of difficulty.

Inspiration theory cannot account for the production of the writings and the diversity of operations behind the writings. It is simply misguided to take the prophet as the model of inspiration. What happens when that is done is that a stereotype is produced, not based on Saul, Samuel and the ecstatic prophets but on the later writing prophets who said, 'The word of Yahweh came to me. Hear the word of Yahweh.' You cannot base an explanation on what may be true of a limited experience of a few of the prophets. For the prophet accounts for only a small portion of Scripture. You also must consider the relation between *Kings* and *Chronicles*, how Luke researched and Paul cogitated. He wrote 'on this I have no word of the Lord' (*I Corinthians* 7:25) but what he said is nevertheless Scripture! To take the prophet as the model of inspiration means that many biblical books are by definition not inspired, and so excluded! They were not produced as the theory says. But such books, for example *Luke, Romans, Galatians,* have had very great influence, and so very great authority.

The problem of the canon is that of how it came that the community accepted certain books and rejected others. Canonisation is a long process. Some members of the community read and accepted some books and a list of books so read and accepted gets drawn up and is itself accepted, and *goes on being accepted.* The writings, of course, circulated separately, not bound together as a whole. The idea of 'the Bible' as a one volume collection is a modern idea. Various collections were made. Why, in the interests of a theory of inspiration, should one accept the traditional decision about sixty-six books? It is hardly an intelligent decision if one has not read some of the other books which eventually were not put in, for example *Didache, Shepherd of Hermas, Epistles of Clement* or is not aware that some of the books which were eventually included were seriously questioned, for example, *Hebrews, Revelation, II Peter.*

The pertinent fact is that a particular book came to have influence. The church accepted it. The book has authority as it is used, as it authorized practice and teaching, whether it is inspired or not. We must therefore examine carefully the usage of the Christian communities. Here three interesting facts emerge. First, usage is selective. Some books are used more than others. Some are not used at all, or hardly at all. If the reader makes a survey over a period of time from within the reader's own community, this will become very plain, as to usage in the reader's community. Second, the books have influence in worship and in devotion. They stimulate and fortify faith. Third, they are appealed to for construction of doctrinal systems, often in conflict with one another.

(4) Our fourth thesis is that revised theories of inspiration are open to serious objection, first in that they are unable to explain what must be explained, and second, that in reworking the theory and seeming to retain the idea of inspiration as central, what results is

actually no longer a theory of *inspiration*. It is one in name only. From this we conclude that inspiration theory cannot provide grounds for an assertion of the authority of the Bible in our time.

Alan Richardson wrote,

> 'What the nineteenth century had not yet realized, if Sanday's work may be taken as its culminating point, was that the non-biblical category of inspiration cannot provide a satisfactory basis for the restatement of the truth concerning the authority of the Bible in the age of science.'[4]

We have in mind in particular the theories of William Sanday (1894) and Bruce Vawter (1972). By discussing issues raised by Sanday we can illustrate in the modern historical context some of the major points outlined above.

The eighteenth and nineteenth centuries had produced significant results in many spheres relevant to the study and assessment of the Bible:

(1) The development of historical analysis and its use in the study of the sources of the biblical literature. We know, as the framers of inspiration theory did not know, how the books came to be produced.

(2) The production of 'Lives' of Jesus, what Schweitzer called the magnificent failure of German biblical scholarship of the nineteenth century. All the 'Lives' are different, even though based on the same sources, the Gospels.

(3) The confrontation between science and Christian belief. Specifically, such questions were discussed as the age of the earth, the fixity of species, the relation of change to purpose, the interpretation of

Scripture, the nature of the truth and relevance of Scripture, the origins of man.

William Sanday (in 1893) spoke at the end of a century of painstaking analytic study of the Bible and, in his book entitled *Inspiration*, he took account of the results of the work in historical analysis of the Bible. Sanday believed that he could establish the authority of the Bible on the basis of its inspiration (1,3). He thus produced a revised theory of inspiration. The following are the chief points.

Inspiration is not a quality which can be predicated of the Bible as a whole and in general. It is present in different degrees in different books (400).

Such inspiration is a quality, a property of the literature.

Inspiration is also a process (as well as the product), and points to a 'superintending Mind' (391-2, 402). In short, inspiration is limited to the empirical process and to the quality of the text that results.

The process accords with what we know about the world, nature and history. There is nothing violent, mechanical. There is no supernatural intervention. The human element is always present (423-4). The only question at issue between the older theory of inspiration and the inductive theory (Sanday's), Sanday admits in a moment of candour, is the *extent* of the human element (423). Sanday's account gives due consideration, as the traditional theory did not, to the human element.

But he has now touched the nerve of the traditional theory which was that God did intervene. God took the initiative, influencing the 'writer' to bring about a result which otherwise would not have happened. God heightened the consciousness of the prophet. God imbued him with thoughts or perhaps words. Something happened to him which does not happen to the rest of us, ordinary mortals or run-of-the-mill believers. God influenced him by providing him the content of which he will write.

This is of course the right procedure. You look at the evidence first. You then construct an explanation which takes all the evidence adequately into account. You ask, for example, 'How does the evidence establish how the writings came into being and were accepted?' The reverse process is wrong procedure. You cannot appeal to inspiration to tell you the answers to questions which only appropriate evidence can supply. Specifically you cannot and must not say, The Bible is inspired, so the writers cannot have borrowed materials from any other sources. Whether the writer borrowed is a matter which only a study of the evidence can establish. So you must take notice of the results of source criticism *before* making judgments about how the writers used sources, not pronounce a judgment in advance of studying the evidence, because your theory demands that judgment. That is prejudice. If one dismisses the results of source criticism in advance, one's judgment (whatever it is) is untrustworthy, since important evidence has been neglected. One of the central questions for Sanday in 1893 was the extent of the human element in the process of 'writing.'

He cannot determine the extent of the human element in advance of the evidence. How does one distinguish the thoughts that press in one's mind — those that are God-given and those which one thinks up oneself? That is why his writing has its 'authority', its

Seventh-Day Adventists and the Bible

set-apartness, its ought-to-be-taken-notice-of-ness. It's there and it's different. He examines the literature, asking careful historical questions and only then draws conclusions about the form which the divine self-communication has taken. For Sanday there is no question about and, it seems, no further problem with, the divine activity. God reveals himself. A reasonable theory of inspiration takes account of the human element. It is by examining the evidence that we discover how the human element plays its part in the total process of revelation.[5]

How then did the Bible come into being? What can we say about the activity which produced this book? The process is in accordance with what we know about the world, about nature and history, specifically about how literary productions come into being and have an influence on a community. When God works there is

> 'nothing violent, nothing mechanical, nothing really sudden, however much it may appear so, but a long concatenation and subtlest interweaving of causes, all knit together as if in a living organism.' (423)

In this complex process, weak human instruments carry forward the divine design (footnote 424).

Earlier, Sanday argued that earlier writers in asserting the authority of the Bible did not discriminate between divine activity and human activity. The older theory held that God took control of the 'writer' and produced the words of Scripture. The human counted for little in the process. The older theory held that all the Scriptures were divinely inspired so that the words of men were in fact the words of God. Thus in the theory the infallibility of the whole was a condition of

Scripture's authority. Inspiration, on this account, described how it could be that the words of men were the very words of God.

Sanday insists that a recognition of the human element is essential for an adequate understanding of the status of the Bible. That has become so widely accepted a principle that it seems anachronistic now to assert it. All human products are relative. Historical judgments about the Bible are of the same sort as are made about all other history.

Sanday expresses his reluctance to pursue the implications of what he has proposed. There is thus an .ncompleteness and tentativeness about his statements on inspiration. But there is no tentativeness about the validity and the fruitfulness of the critical historical method of biblical study. In this he contrasts with Benjamin Jowett, who a third of a century earlier,[6] feels called upon to defend the historical method and to comment, even to plead for, the openness of mind to accept it and to give sympathetic consideration to the conclusions it leads to. Thirty-four years had made some difference,

Sanday did not feel called upon to provide a systematic theory of inspiration He says so much when claiming but not further explaining that the utterances of the prophets had an objective cause outside the prophet (146). So some of his teachings are assertions rather than explanations. We shall not misrepresent him if we simply list his basic convictions.

1. Prophetic inspiration is the type of all inspiration (128, 268).

2. The utterances of the prophet (and so it would seem of those others of whom he prophet was a type)

have a source outside themselves (146). Hence we may say that the words were 'not merely their own inventions.'[7] Should we or should we not call this 'verbal inspiration'? How are we to think of this happening?

3. The process over a long period is revelation. Revelation is progressive (164).

4. The inspiration of the prophet, while customarily typical (cf. 1. above), is not always typical. For example, psalmists, wise men, historians had an inspiration 'of their own' (263). The inspiration of the prophet did not 'supersede' the ordinary use of historical materials. (Does not this ambiguity call for explanation?)

5. Inspiration did not prevent the possibility of error by 'interfering with' the 'ordinary use of historical materials' (269).

6. In the New Testament, inspiration extends from the single truth to the system of truth, 'a body of connected truths, a system of thought' (353). This is the 'more sustained character of the apostolic inspiration' (354).

7. The divine acts through the human (355), both through the reception by the individual and in the process of collection and presentation.

8. The extent of the human activity is to be discovered through empirical investigation and not to be asserted *a priori*. This is a particular concern of the inductive theory (423).

9. The authority of the Bible no longer depends upon an *a priori*, that is a dogmatic, assertion of the divine origin of the writings and upon a failure to distinguish the divine from the human. To assert the

authority of the Bible does not depend upon its being infallible. The genuine humanity of the authors is taken into account. This means that we are now able to discriminate between the divine and the human elements in the process of inspiration (425). (This cannot be left as an assertion. It requires explanation).

10. The process by which God reveals himself includes the human and has respect for the interrelation of natural and human causes. There is no gate-crashing into history or into nature (425).

11. The inspiration of the Bible is the basis for asserting the authority of the Bible (1,3).

We shall now take issue with this primary position of Sanday (11).

'The Bible is inspired' does not mean 'The Bible has authority.' 'The Bible is the inspired Word of God,' is the basic statement of any theory of inspiration. But it is ambiguous and hence unclear. It is because it is unclear that it can, and often readily is, given a meaning congenial to a particular theological viewpoint. In a word, the statement, 'The Bible is the inspired Word of God' is often equated with the statement 'The Bible has special authority.' I do not believe they are equivalent. Nor does it follow from 'The Bible is inspired' that 'The Bible has authority.' The claim that the Bible has authority will have to be established separately from the claim that the Bible is inspired. The claim that the Bible is inspired must be clearly defined before we even know what we are saying.

There are two alternatives. It might mean either The Bible is the having-been-inspired Word of God, or The Bible is the now inspired Word of God.

The very point of discussions of inspiration is to show that the product (the Bible) has a unique history, to indicate the divine activity in the process of its production. It is, it is argued, a unique book because it came into being in a special way, by the 'inspiration' of God upon the 'writer.' Once *that* has been asserted, claims about the product are then made on that basis. The argument runs: Because God has inspired the writer and the writing (past tense), the product of that process is unique, set apart, inerrant etc. But if that is what is meant, when the claim is made 'The Bible is inspired (present tense)', we are attaching a quite different meaning to the idea of 'inspired.' 'Inspired' now means 'special,' 'inerrant,' 'authoritative,' and that is *not* the same meaning as 'produced by a process in which the Spirit of God operates.' It is either a separate assertion, or it is a deduction. The first statement is a statement about a process in the past. The second is a statement about a status in the present, when that process is complete.

So what is one saying when one says that the Bible *is* inspired, in contrast to saying that the 'writer' *was* inspired, or the process *was* inspired? Two things: (1) one is attributing certain qualities to the book, and (2) one is recommending rules for its use. Such rules are: This book is to authorise beliefs and practices. Use this book as a basis for deducing a system of doctrine and then believe the system.

For the traditional theory to say that the Bible is inspired means that it discloses truths about God not available elsewhere; that it is authoritative, equally and in all its parts; that it is exempt from error.[8]

But, if that is what one wants to say, why use the term *inspiration*? It is quite meaningful when used of the psychological state of the 'writer' and can express the conviction that the source of that state and of the writing that issued from it was divine. It then suggests a parallel to other such phenomena, for example the mantic phenomena of Greek soothsayers and oracles. But that is not a biblical idea.

To use the term 'inspired' to express the claim that the Bible is authoritative is to assume 'is inspired' and 'has authority' are univocal i.e. have identical meaning. That just cannot be assumed. One cannot establish the authority of the Bible by giving an account of the process by which it came to be written. 'The writer and the process was inspired' can be given a reasonably clear meaning. 'The Bible (the product) is inspired' does not add anything to that meaning. It is difficult in fact to say clearly what it does mean. It is clear that it *intends* to say something else. 'The Bible (the product) is inspired' intends to say something more than 'the writer was inspired.' That is the issue: *whether it does or does not say anything more.* The traditional theory has to add other terms, so talk about inerrancy, infallibility, self-authentication. It has to invent new terms by putting qualifiers before 'inspiration.' So it speaks of 'plenary inspiration,' 'verbal inspiration,' 'thought inspiration.' These terms are confusing, since one in not sure whether they are intended to refer to the process or to the product. Whether they describe how the book came to be, or qualities of the book, once produced. Indeed they refer in different ways to both. What was produced in this way has a special character because it was so produced.[9] We are meant to understand by the expression

Seventh-Day Adventists and the Bible 53

'The Bible is inspired' not simply how it came about but that it has a special status and authority. We are expected to accept the transition from the one to the other. But we must ask whether this is a verbal trick, which seeks to make the term 'inspired' bear a meaning which it does not, cannot and should not bear. To move from the one statement to the other means establishing the first assertion and providing a convincing argument to make plausible the movement from the first to the second assertion. Both of these are suspect.

To establish the first assertion we hear talk of God 'taking hold' of the 'writer' so that what is written is what God wanted written. That is a very misleading account of how the Bible was produced. But let us suppose, for the sake of argument, that God has got via the writer what God wants written down. That does not mean, and does not show, that the writing has authority. Because God is the source of a set of statements does not mean nor imply that those statements have authority.

To say so is to commit a category mistake. That mistake is in saying that the writings have something else called 'authority' other than the influence and esteem they have in the community. The mistake is in referring to a supposed something other than the presence of the divine reality they mediate, to something extra which the writings 'contain'!

> 'A doctrine about scripture's 'inspiration' is not identical with a doctrine about its 'authority,' 'Authority' cannot mean 'divinely inspired.' 'Inspiration' is a property of texts, while 'authority' is a relational term . . . . Given a doctrine of scripture's 'authority', i.e. how scripture ought

concretely to be used and construed in the common life of the church and in doing theology, a doctrine of 'inspiration' gives a theological explanation of why, when scripture is used in that way, certain results sometimes follow.'[11]

What follows from this is quite simple.

(1) You can show that the Bible has authority without developing (dubious) theories of inspiration.
(2) To establish the authority of a document for a community in the present, you must ask what status it has in the present and what it does in the present. You must ask in relation to what and for whom it has the status is has and does what it does.
(3) No account of how the book came to be what it now is can explain why it has authority in the present, if it does. All the having-been-inspired books might have been forgotten, have fallen into disuse or been lost. They would then be having-been-inspired and non-authoritative. On the other hand, books which were not said to have-been-inspired might be exercising a very real influence in the present. So the question, 'How does it come to exercise authority?' and 'Was it inspired or not?' are two quite different questions. If there is some connection between them it will have to be shown. We cannot assume such a connection.[12] It would not be reasonable to do so.

'It surely cannot be supposed that to call scripture 'authority' means that properly employed it could 'guarantee' the correctness of our proposals, if only we could figure out how to employ it correctly.[13]

No doctrinal position is able to tell us how to use scripture so as to guarantee that God will be present to illumine and to correct us. This overlooks the essential importance of (1) the presence of the Holy Spirit. It also overlooks the fact that (2) the interpreter moves from the text of the Bible to the concrete situation of the church by using quite particular procedures of interpretation. He selects end relates what he selects from the Bible to the doctrinal or theological schemes he works out, and does so in specifiable ways. He does not normally simply repeat or 'translate' the biblical language. 'Transposition' is not an adequate term either to describe the construction that theology involves.

A reference to God, the Holy Spirit, reminds the Christian that he is not dealing only with a text. What authority the Bible has, it has because God reveals himself through it.

We must relate the statement that the Bible is the authority for the church to the further claim that God, as he manifests himself, is the absolute authority. This means that God, through Christ, through the Holy Spirit is active in the life and activity of the church in the present. The two claims must be brought together. To know the truth means being involved in and influenced by this activity of God.

It is therefore important to address ourselves to the question, 'In what sense exactly the scriptures are the revelation of God and the standard of faith.'[14] So we leave behind us accounts of the process by which the books of the Bible came to be produced and compiled. It is just sheer naiveté to think you can simply move from claims about inspiration of writings in the past to claims about authority in the present.

There is only one way in which one may appear to do this. That is to extend the meaning of the term 'inspiration' to the event that happens in the present when the writings become the instrument of God's revelation in the church and in the world. One might then make some analogies or comparisons between what sometimes happened when the writings came into being and what is happening with them as they function within the church in the present. The word 'inspiration' is now being extended to cover the Bible's function as the medium of God's revelation in the present. But that very clearly *is* an extension of the meaning of the term, deliberately made to connect the idea of inspiration with that of authority. Since this cannot be done unless one speaks of God's revealing himself, through the Scriptures, in the present time, *the key idea is that of revelation rather than inspiration.* This idea has shown itself to be very much more fruitful than that of inspiration in this connection.[15]

A good example is to be found in the book on inspiration by the Catholic, Bruce Vawter. In setting out his own constructive statement he argues that we should extend the meaning of the concept of inspiration. So he writes (and we select just two extracts):

'Both Protestant and Catholic thinking have conspired to a growing recognition that biblical inspiration in the narrow sense, the sense in which it has generally been subjected to ecclesiastical pronouncements and the examination of theologians, is but one stage in the unfolding of a mystery of communication that encompasses earlier and later stages as well.'

'Luther, it might appear, was posing the question as it ought to have been posed all along; in relation to a dynamic and living as opposed to a static and fossilized inspired, word. That is to say, if the role of the word in the church was to be seen less as archival testimony and more as the continuing presence of the Spirit — the way, we have seen, that the Bible itself understood the word — then the inspirational process itself ought to be considered not as merely terminating in a literary text but as touching also the later reader and hearer of the word. For word is not properly word, not the means of communication and revelation until it has been taken in, until the process of communicating is thereby completed. When we are dealing with an inspired word, then, inspiration should be regarded as proper to every stage of communication.'[16]

We can readily agree with much of what is expressed here: the coming into being of the books is one stage in a complex process; the book is living word and not a dead, 'fossilized,' letter; the process is not complete until the word has been received. The question is how we shall express those important convictions. Vawter wishes to extend the reference of the term 'inspiration' to the later reception of the word, indeed, to 'every stage of communication.' This we must reject. The reason is that it is to place too wide a range of meanings on the term 'inspiration.' It would be more appropriate to use a related but more versatile conception, that of revelation. It can serve better the goals that Vawter has in mind, which are, (1) to point to a process of divine initiative in the production of the book; (2) to indicate a divine presence in relation to the use of scripture; (3) to insist on the importance of the receiving of the word and to relate that as the goal of the whole process to the activity of the Holy Spirit.

In view of the ways in which the term 'inspiration' has been used in the past, I believe that it is unsuitable to attempt to extend its meaning in this way. One could use the term *theopneustia*, but again confusion and unclarity would result. The fact is that the doctrine of inspiration has been in protestant theology 'for the most a part a chapter of accidents.'[17] It became a fossilized doctrine. It became abstracted from the most important data concerning the Bible: namely its potential ineffectiveness as mere letter when isolated from the 'testimony of the Holy Spirit'; its genuine humanity; and its errancy. The theory of inspiration focussed upon the letter and gave scant room to the reality which imparted to the letter the life it has within the church.

Seventh-day Adventists as well as being concerned about the Bible have traditionally had a further interest in inspiration. The basic arguments used in regard to the Bible and the basic but grossly inflated concept of 'the prophet' are used without change of Ellen White. Specifically the fundamental argument from inspiration to authority is here used, as follows:

E.G.White was inspired. Therefore the writings of E.G.White are inspired. Therefore, the writings of E.G.White have authority.

The form of argument is identical in both cases. So is the definition of inspiration and the conception of authority. This means that on the basis of these definitions, this conception and this argument we cannot distinguish between *the status* of the Bible and the status of the writings of E.G.White. Is the distinction then a formal one, and one not borne out in fact by the actual practice of the church? Or is it just an historical accident that E.G.White was a nineteenth century American on the stage of church history at a particular time and place?

We have seen that it is community usage that defines what authority a body of writings has in that community. Are they read and quoted widely and continuously? Is notice taken of them in particular? Is time and effort taken in relating the writings to the doctrinal scheme and to church practice? Are they well circulated compared to other books, the Bible included, and to theological authors? Answers to these and similar questions will indicate the currency and hence authority E.G.White has and has had in the church.

Now is it not clearer, more straightforward, indeed more honest to say, 'This is what we *do* with E.G.White in this community'; 'This is what we expect you to do with E.G.White,' than to try to buttress the insistence that E.G.White be read, followed and revered (which for many people means as much a psychological and social as a rational commitment) with indefensible arguments and claims about inspiration. For as we have seen even if a writer were inspired and even if books were produced from divine origin as the theory demands, that neither establishes nor guarantees their authority.

The function of the theory of the inspiration of E.G.White, as with that of the Bible, is two-fold: first, to attempt to provide rational grounds for a position already taken, and for the use of the materials. A theory of inspiration was available to hand, having been developed in reference to the Bible by the Protestant scholastics, and having some popular currency during the nineteenth century. It was transferred, *mutatis mutandis*, to

E.G.White for the purpose of establishing or of confirming E. G. White's authority. Seventh-day Adventist writers in the late nineteenth century could find and incorporate statements and arguments about inspiration from Christian writers. E. G. White did it herself. But that was more than a century ago. The second function was and is to provide what we shall call a regula derectiva, a rule for use, an imperative. E. G. White was inspired. The writings of E. G. White are inspired. Therefore, treat them as primary authorities. Act as if they were not relative (hence the pother about borrowing, plagiarism, other people's composition and editing. Hence also the discussion whether E.G.White is not, in reality, the primary source, rather than the Bible). Use the writings as primary sources for piety, for guidance in moral matters and in doctrinal construction, for direction in church affairs. Connect what you teach and everything you teach with E.G.White, then follow what you teach. In short, Teach what E.G.White teaches. Do what E.G.White says ought to be done.

Here theory is fundamental. Put bluntly, the theory overrides all other considerations. You do not need to look at the facts. Inspiration, having taken place, is the guarantee, even in advance of the evidence regarding the composition, veracity and status of the writings.

What this all means is that it is no loss to abandon the inspiration theory. The writings of E.G.White might then be seen and evaluated as historical documents, related to particular times and places, to personal and social contexts and to the actual development of an ecclesiastical community, with its limitations, shortsightedness, with its mistakes and wrong turnings as well as its successes and triumphs. It is their historical location in that development which sets the writings apart. We have learned that this is true of course of the New Testament.

The authority of a literature cannot be asserted in isolation from its history. Such historical placement represents emancipation from prejudice and the a priori judgment. Our place today in the historical development is different and demands new discussion, the assessment of old positions and old priorities. Here we may gain help from outside the immediate ecclesiastical sources, and put the provincial discussion in a wider context, with salutary results.

Notes

[1] Cf. Peter Hodgson and Robert King, *Christian Theology*. Philadelphia: Fortress Press, 1982. pp. 93-96.

[2] James Barr, *Fundamentalism*. London: S.C.M. Press, 1981. pp. 289-291. Barr finds fundamentalists' denial of dictation as the mode of God's communication to be inconsistent, in J.I. Packer, for example They do not, he suggests, want to be saddled with too big a miracle. They want to be modern, but at the same time cannot bear the implications of the analytical questions which may be raised about the composition of the writings.

For an example of such writings cf. J. J Packer, *Fundamentalism and the Word of God.* London: Intervarsity Fellowship, 1958, especially chapter IV. Scripture. pp. 75-114.. Dewey N. Beegle, *The Inspiration of Scripture.* Philadelphia: Westminster Press, 1963. Carl F.H.Henry, *Revelation and the Bible.*

Philadelphia: Presbyterian and Reformed Publishing Company, 1958. Robert Preuss, *The Inspiration of Scripture. A Study of the Theology of the 17th. Century Lutheran Dogmaticians.* Edinburgh: Oliver and Boyd, 1957. William Sanday, *Inspiration*. London: Longmans Green and Co. Third Edition, 1901. D. Guthrie, 'The Authority of Scripture,' in *The New Bible Commentary Revised.* London: Inter-varsity Press, 1976. Cf. bibliography in James Barr, *op. cit.*, pp. 363ff.

[3]B.B.Warfield, *The Inspiration and Authority of the Bible.* Philadelphia: The Presbyterian and Reformed Publishing Co., 1948, p.210. Cf. Alan Richardson, *The Bible in the Age of Science*, London: S.C.M. Press, 1968. p. 73. Benjamin Jowett, 'On the Interpretation of Scripture,' in *Essays and Reviews*, Seventh edition. London: Longman Green, Longman and Roberts, 1961. p. 351. David H. Kelsey, *The Uses of Scripture in Recent Theology.* London: S.C.M. Press, 1975. p. 21. Jowett said, 'The question of inspiration is to the interpreter as though it were not important.' *Ibid.*

[4]Alan Richardson, *op. cit.*, pp. 75-76

[5]William Sanday, *Inspiration*. References in the text are to this book, published a year after the lectures. Sanday does not use the term 'revelation' frequently. When he does, he uses it in two senses, of what is revealed (423) and of the activity of revealing (424). That represents the familiar distinction between *revaluate* and *revelation*.

[6]Benjamin Jowett, *op. cit.* Jowett can point to the fallacy of accepting a theory of inspiration as providing rules for interpreting scripture such as: any passage can be co-ordinated with any other passage; take everything in the Bible as true; raise no 'critical' questions. Jowett

denies that we can now rest doctrines on texts of scripture, simply co-ordinating passages which appear to contain similar words or ideas (p. 421).

He can also say that a theory of inspiration has no relation to interpretation, so that the interpreter can for all intents and purposes ignore it (p. 351).

The fact is that Jowett speaks of interpretation on two levels. In one case, the interpreter seeks to get at what the 'writer' meant, to get at the intention of the author. 'The true use of interpretation is to get rid of interpretation, and leave us alone in company with the author' (p. 384). In the other case there is construction of doctrine in relation to Scripture. Jowett recognizes the difficulty of this latter task, but says no more about it. While he is concerned with the first level of interpretation, the problems of the second are always in his mind. The issues are complex.

[7] 'The words which they (the prophets) repeat and the visions of revelation which they describe are not merely their own inventions, but are suggested and brought home to them from without in such a way that they were irresistibly attributed to God and given out as coming from him.' Sanday, *op. cit*, p. 147.

[8] Cf. Sanday, *op.cit.*, pp. 392-393.

[9] The argument that is needed to establish this conclusion runs as follows: God indited the words, the thoughts. So the product is true, representative of God's will as is no other document. So it has unequalled authority. So it must be followed, obeyed, believed.

[10] A category mistake occurs when we apply ideas which are appropriate in one sphere of discourse to another subject matter where they are not appropriate. A

category mistake occurs when ideas are wrongly used put in a context where they do not belong. Concepts must be deployed properly. Such category mistakes are made by people who do not know how to wield concepts in the right way. So puzzles arise due to 'inability to use certain items of the English vocabulary'. *Cf.* Gilbert Ryle, *The Concept of Mind.* London: Hutchinson, 1949. p. 17. Ryle's particular target is the 'para-mechanical hypothesis' which speaks of mind, or soul, as an entity in addition to the body and separable from it. It is a category mistake because it speaks of what is the function, the operation of the whole organism as requiring a separate entity. The soul or mind is not another thing in addition to the body. It would be a category mistake if I were to say, 'Well! I've seen Washington, New York, North Carolina, San Francisco, Yellowstone, Nashville, but now I would like to see America.' America is not something in addition to these places. Your answer to me would be, 'You've seen it already!'

The believer reads the Bible. It gives him understanding, direction. The church reads the Bible. It gives it understanding, direction. For the Christian the scripture mediates the reality of God, his demands, life, succour, the reality of Jesus Christ. The category mistake is to think of the authority of the Bible as something else, something other, something in addition to this.

The Bible mediates the presence of God in the community of Christians in that it is the instrument for the revealing of Jesus Christ. That happens. To this event the Christian can and does testify. But testimony is not demonstration. The mistake is to give reason to 'establish' the authority of scripture. So what are the reasons purporting to establish such authority? They are such as the following: the Bible claims to have authority; Jesus used scripture and claimed it had authority; the church teaches that the scriptures have authority; what the Bible says is factually true; the predictions made in the Bible come true; the apostles had authority and they acknowledged the authority of the 'Old Testament' writings; the miracles of the Bible have their source in God; the 'writers' of the Bible were inspired; the Bible is a book written by spiritual experts; the doctrinal system requires the authority of the Bible.

Such reasons do not provide adequate grounds to establish the kind of authority which the Bible distinctively has, neither individually nor taken all together. The sort of authority the Bible has is not established, and cannot be established, by giving reasons, by providing arguments.. The category mistake lies here. The error is not that one has not given the right reasons. It is that one tries to *establish* the authority of the Bible by providing reasons. There is no question of providing a logical demonstration of such authority.

[11]David H. Kelsey, *The Uses of Scripture in Recent Theology*, p.211.

[12]People may come to acknowledge the uniqueness of the Bible, because they have accepted that it was inspired. What we have shown is that that acknowledgement is questionable on the grounds claimed by the traditional account of inspiration. It overlooks the important function of argument in the process, and does not establish the unique *religious* authority the Bible has for the believer. The Bible is for the believer primarily a spiritual, a religious book. The

believer testifies to its influence and function. He does not and cannot demonstrate an external authority by argument.

[13] Kelsey, *op. cit.*, p. 215.

[14] H.H.Farmer, 'The Bible: Its Significance and Authority,' in *The Interpreter's Bible*, Vol. I, New York and Nashville: Abingdon Press, 1952. pp. 3-31. The quotation is from p. 3.

[15] We cannot pursue this further here. It was Martin Kähler who, reacting against the 'Lives of Jesus' movement and its handling of the Gospel sources, insisted that the Bible is the book which mediates the reality of God for the Christian believer. The 'Christ of faith' was at the centre of the very being of the church. The Bible is primarily a religious book. The purpose of the writing 'is to awaken faith in Jesus Christ through a clear-cut proclamation of his saving activity.' That is particularly true of the Gospels, which is the special concern of Kähler, and of much scholarship of the nineteenth and twentieth centuries. M.Kähler, *The So-called Historical Jesus and the Historic Biblical Christ*. Translated by Carl E. Braaten. Philadelphia: Fortress Press, 1964. See especially pp. 100-148. The quotation is from p. 127.

[16] Bruce Vawter, *Biblical Inspiration*. London: Hutchinson, 1972. pp. 158, 78-79.

[17] Karl Barth, *Church Dogmatics, I/2*, Translated by G.T. Thomson and Harold Knight. Edinburgh: T& T Clark, 1970. p. 526.

Lightning Source UK Ltd.
Milton Keynes UK
UKHW011823090920
369608UK00001B/159